UNDER HIS SHADOW
WRITINGS
Volume 3

by David Mayorga

Published by

SHABAR PUBLICATIONS
www.shabarpublications.com

Most Shabar Publications products are available at special quantity discounts for bulk purchase for sales promotions, fund-raising and educational needs. For details, write Shabar Publications at mayorga1126@gmail.com.

Under His Shadow Writings Volume 3 *by David Mayorga*
Published by Shabar Publications
3833 N. Taylor Rd.
Palmhurst, Texas 78573
www.shabarpublications.com
www.masterbuildertx.com

This book or parts thereof may not be reproduced in any form, stored in a retrieval system, or transmitted in any form by any means - electronic, mechanical, photocopy, recording, or otherwise - without prior written permission of the publisher, except as provided by United States of America copyright law.

Unless otherwise noted, all Scripture quotations are from the New Kings James Version of the Bible. Copyright@1979, 1980, 1982 by Thomas Nelson, Inc., publishers. Used by permission.

Edited by Emily Rose King

Copyright @ 2022 by David Mayorga

All rights reserved.

ISBN 978-1-955433-08-2

Table of Contents

Introduction 5
Day 1: In God-ALL Slow Starts, End Well! 8
Day 2: Have You Been Taken Captive? 11
Day 3: When the Time is Completed! 14
Day 4: Does God Know About It? 18
Day 5: God's Intent is to Rebuild Us! 21
Day 6: God's Eternal Cord! 25
Day 7: Know and Understand the Season You Are In! ...29
Day 8: Why Does God Allow Calamities In My Life? 32
Day 9: Learn to Refresh Others! 36
Day 10: Do You Believe In the Impossible? 39
Day 11: Welcome to the Inaccessible! 42
Day 12: Downloads of Revelation! 46
Day 13: Going a Little Father! 49
Day 14: A Word from the Lord! 52
Day 15: It Was Fitting! 55
Day 16: The Ministry of Life in Living Color! 58
Day 17: Vision of Man in Captivity! 61
Day 18: Today, If You Hear His Voice! 64
Day 19: God, Help Me Enter into Your Dreams! 67

Day 20: His Way and How To Walk It Out! 70
Day 21: Pierced by His Word! 73
Day 22: Rightly Corrected! 76
Day 23: A Time for the Sword! 79
Day 24: Recognizing Opportunity! 82
Day 25: Tipped Over! 87
Day 26: The Promise Keeper! 91
Day 27: Never Look for the Easy Way! 94
Day 28: Failing Strength! 97
Day 29: Only Through Jesus! 100
Day 30: To Do Your Will Oh God! 103
Day 31: The Soul Who Seeks Him! 106
Day 32: Hold Fast to Jesus! 109
Day 33: A Rewarding Confidence! 112
Day 34: Acceptable Content! 116
Day 35: Can't Please Him, If 119
Day 36: I Know What the Promise is Not! 123
Day 37: When God Begs to Differ! 126
Day 38: A Tool, An Experience, or A Pasison? 130
Day 39: Can You See Him Who Is Invisible? 134
Day 40: God's Watchman! 137
Ministry Information 140

Introduction

"When they had twisted a crown of thorns, they put it on His head, and a reed in His right hand. And they bowed the knee before Him and mocked Him, saying, 'Hail, King of the Jews!' Then they spat on Him and took the reed and struck Him on the head. And when they had mocked Him, they took the robe off Him, put His own clothes on Him, and led Him away to be crucified. Now as they came out, they found a man of Cyrene, Simon by name. Him they compelled to bear His cross." (Matthew 27:29-32)

Entering this new year, the Holy Spirit began to challenge me to see Jesus in everything. What do I mean by this? I mean that we look at life through the eyes of Christ. Everything that happens in our lives— yes, the good and the bad, they are all processed by Christ. Nothing can touch us unless the Lord has allowed it!

Establishing our spiritual lives in the light of eternity is call for every believer. To see life from God's perspective is really the key to a successful life in God. Christians are still pursuing their own agenda. They are still praying and asking God to bless their plans when the Lord never initiated them. If we haven't gotten a hold of this yet, it is time we did— God will only bless those things He initiates!

It is my intention to write with the passion I have felt for years. It is my heart's desire to set your heart on fire! No apologies. While some are still playing games on God's borrowed time, some of us have literally taken God seriously. Have you?

For my fasting prayer time, I have come to the Lord with nothing but a yielded heart and spirit. I have no agenda but only what He allows me to say and do. Christ must once again be first and foremost. He must be the only reason for every season! Christ must increase and I must decrease, to use John the Baptist's wonderful words.

It is my belief that Christianity without the cross of Christ in it, is a powerless religion.. Unless we are willing to go to the cross and die daily, we will be powerless rendering us ineffective in the world we live in.

All power, authority, and wisdom comes from Him! If He is not the One occupying our hearts, then we are allowing our flesh to take over!

The flesh has always found a way to subtly take over our lives by lulling us to sleep with its flashy ideas, promising concepts, and insidious innovations. Repeatedly, when we cease praying, we don't only fall asleep, but also the enemy moves in with intention to kill us!

My prayer for this next 40 days of prayer and fasting is that your heart will be stirred and warmed by His glory. Also, let me just say that if we are not readying ourselves for dying to self, we are by default, readying ourselves for compromising, corruption, and consequently for collapsing!

David Mayorga, *Author*
McAllen, Texas

Day 1

In God – ALL Slow Starts, End Well!

**"Those who sow in tears
Shall reap in joy.
He who continually goes forth weeping,
Bearing seed for sowing,
Shall doubtless come again with rejoicing,
Bringing his sheaves with him."** (Psalm 126:5, 6)

Woke up this morning to meet God in prayer and the Spirit of the Lord began to stir my heart in very powerful ways.

First, I want to say to you that I wasn't feeling well this morning during my prayer time. I felt my body as if it was fighting a cold or something, but the feeling seemed very overwhelming for a while.

As I continued praying and breaking through, a couple of things came to my mind: One of them was all the celebration that people were experiencing the night before, being that it was New Year's Eve; and secondly, the voice of the enemy speaking to me and saying, Everyone is happy and go-lucky and look at you, - you are sick, sad, and fasting!

The enemy continued in saying what an unfortunate time for seeking God. The devil suggested that maybe I should postpone my protracted fast for a better time when I was feeling strong and focused. Though it sounded like good advice, I know the devil too well. He was making a case for my flesh!

It was here where the Spirit of the Lord broke through with such an awesome revelation and a Scripture for the coming year. Let me share some of this with you.

Sowing in Tears!

Sowing in tears is a figurative way of saying you are going through hell, but God will take you out of that furnace shortly— just be patient and wait and see! The Scripture in Psalm 126:5, 6, goes on to say that those who sow in tears, will reap in joy. There is a time for reaping. Though the situation didn't start off good or the new venture didn't kick off as well as you thought, if we remain faithful in the Lord, He will get us to our desired end.

Continual Weeping Produces Life!

Continual weeping is God's way of producing life in us. It is here where His seeds are produced in us. As we go forth weeping, we are producing seeds (in the spirit). Obviously, people who see us going through the process may tend to feel sorry for us. Yet in the end, we will come home with our sheaves!

As I close this devotion, let me just say, God will never let us down. If we put in the tears, He will put in the harvest!

Under His Shadow Prayer

Thinking of a New Year arriving and me abiding in You and You in me, gives me hope and fills my life with expectation of my future. Thank You Jesus for always being my Refuge! Though things appear to start off slow or on the negative, I know that if I keep my eyes upon You – You will turn things around in Your own time! Amen.

As the Scripture says, **"You will keep him in perfect peace, whose mind is stayed on You, because he trusts in You."** (Isaiah 26:3)

Day 2

Have You Been Taken Captive?

"They shall be carried to Babylon, and there they shall be until the day that I visit them,' says the Lord. 'Then I will bring them up and restore them to this place.'" (Jeremiah 27:22)

In our walk with Christ, there will be many times that you and I will be personally dealt by the Lord. Why does the Lord deal with us in such personal ways? It is my conviction that God at various times will come to us personally and speak into our lives with directives, commands, and corrections that will be used to align us to His will and His ways.

It has been my understanding for most of my Christian journey, that God will focus more on our character development, than all the things we want or need from Him.

I know that many believers hold another version of Christianity; it is a Christianity that says, God loves me, and I desire the best! I do believe with all that is within me, that God does love us, and that He desires the best for us, absolutely! But I also believe that before one can experience a resurrection, one must first die to self!

Captivity vs. Bondage!

Captivity is very different from being in bondage. When in captivity, know that the Lord has brought you here for the purpose of protecting and coaching us. Under bondage, one is carried by the enemy for the purpose of serving him through means of slavery.

Captivity is God's way of getting our attention; bondage is the devil's way of destroying our future!

Servants of the Cross!

True servants of the cross of Christ, understand this lifestyle, the lifestyle of a deeper walk in the things of God's Spirit. Knowing that this walk with God is no longer a walk to please the flesh but rather to please God, the servant of God endeavors to sit at the feet of Jesus daily for the sake of taking orders— not giving them!

As we are being led by the Lord into captivity, understand that it is God Himself that will bring us into the captivity; and when the work has been completed, God Himself, will escort us back and restore us to our original place.

It is my belief that we will be more humble, more broken, a lot wiser, and with a renewed passion to follow Jesus wherever He goes!

Under His Shadow Prayer

Lord Jesus, as I pondered these words from Jeremiah, I have come to know and to believe that life happens because of You! As a matter of fact, everything that has been allowed in our lives has come from Your hand. Sometimes, I have been corrected because I have been wayward; other times, You have corrected me because I needed to learn certain principles; and again, at times, I have been corrected because You wanted to instill in me a greater zeal and fear for Your Name! Lord whatever the cost, I will pay it! If captivity is needed in my life oh Lord, I welcome it! Amen.

Day 3

When the Time is Completed!

"For thus says the Lord: After seventy years are completed at Babylon, I will visit you and perform My good word toward you, and cause you to return to this place. For I know the thoughts that I think toward you, says the Lord, thoughts of peace and not of evil, to give you a future and a hope. Then you will call upon Me and go and pray to Me, and I will listen to you. And you will seek Me and find Me, when you search for Me with all your heart. I will be found by you, says the Lord, and I will bring you back from your captivity; I will gather you from all the nations and from all the places where I have driven you, says the Lord, and I will bring you to the place from which I cause you to be carried away captive." (Jeremiah 29:10-14)

As God begins to take our lives into a deeper realm with Him, we will begin to understand that not too many people walk in this divine order. As a matter of fact, I have found most of the so-called church to be caught up in itself and not in Christ. The thought that God would take them into captivity or any type of personal discipline, makes many believers squirm.

In my meditation this morning, I have discovered that the Lord doesn't want us to be so caught up with our pain and struggle. If one focuses much on themselves, they will begin to make themselves an idol and rob God of His glory. One and time again, you will experience countless battles with your inner self; you will learn that there is truly nothing good in you— the only good thing in us is Christ Himself!

When the Years are Completed!

Once the season of testing and discipline (captivity) has ended, the Lord Himself will bring us back to our original place. our lives, however, will be totally reformed from the inside out.

The immature believer who longs to know Christ in deeper ways, will grow weary and impatient with the way God deals with them. They will become irritated by their inability to make any change to their present situation and will start wiggling their way out so that they may escape captivity. Know that when impatience comes in like a flood, it is the Lord working a deep work in us.

A Hope and a Future!

The Scripture goes on to say to us that God has great thoughts regarding us. Some of those thoughts are to give us hope and a future. In other words, our season of captivity is not the end, it is only a means to the end. God has a future, but He knows we are still too self-centered to walk in it, so He purifies us and makes us suitable for the grand prize!

A Changed Prayer Life!

In closing, let me just say that in our captivity, we will learn to talk to God in prayer. We will learn to listen and obey. There is nothing like a good season of captivity, to help us cultivate a richer and more intense prayer life.

As far as outward possessions and blessings, we need not to worry. God will add all those things to our lives as needed—if only we don't make that our only aim!

Under His Shadow Prayer

Heavenly Father, spending my time in Your sweet presence

today, has been such a delight. I know that You are always interested in my spiritual development— for I know that out of it, comes all the issues of life. All wisdom and knowledge from Your word apply to me and my future. Thank you for caring for me the way You do. If I haven't said this to you this morning, I want You to know that I love You Jesus with all that is within me. Thank you for this wonderful life. Amen.

Day 4

Does God Know About It?

"According to the grace of God which was given to me, as a wise master builder I have laid the foundation, and another builds on it. But let each one take heed how he builds on it. For no other foundation can anyone lay than that which is laid, which is Jesus Christ." (1 Corinthians 3:10-11)

While sitting at the Lord's feet this morning, the Holy Spirit came to me and reminded me that though we live in a hurry-hurry world, in a world filled with so much knowledge and countless opportunities for being successful – we must always remember that there is only one foundation to all of this – it is Christ!

All of life flows out of the heart of God. To try and make life happen without God's leadership is surely a plan for great chaos and disaster. One must be wise in dealing with life, is what I think. Don't ever trust your emotions; don't ever trust your intuition as great as you think it might be. Trust the Spirit's leadership. Only He alone can build upon your life, for He knows that Christ is the foundation of your life. He will never take you where Christ won't want you to be!

During my attentiveness to hear God this morning, I heard the Spirit of God say to me: Learn to be sensitive to me David. Learn to hear my voice and hear my gentle steps; learn to follow my rhythm, my timing, and get to know My heart for your life. Your life is not like every life — your life is different from others.

I know our lives all have different blueprints, but in the end we all must give Him all the glory!

Christ the Foundation!

Too often, we tend to embrace good opportunities: jobs, relationships, vocations, financial wisdom, a healthy diet, etc. These are all good, and they will probably help us along the way in our life.

Here's something you want to ponder: What will be the result of these opportunities? You might say, I'll be better off financially, or I will be better health-wise, or how about, I will get to make new friends! If you notice, all these things have to do with self. All these things aggrandize who you are and what you want, but nothing to do with Christ.

We tend to see all these awesome blessings but totally negate His presence or involvement in any of it!

Learn to Be Accountable to God!

If you are truly a follower of Jesus and desire to be led by His Spirit, learn to be accountable to God. When in prayer, ask the Lord why such an opportunity appeared before you. Learn to inquire of the Lord and ask Him what He honestly thinks of it, and/or if it is something that will bring Him glory.

Under His Shadow Prayer

King Jesus, once again I come before you with the need to be realigned in my thinking. I need you to guide me through all the changes that surround me daily. May my spirit always be in tune with Yours! Please allow me to have the sensitivity to hear your footsteps at every turn in this journey. I need you more than ever before Jesus! Amen.

Day 5

God's Intent is to Rebuild Us!

"The Lord has appeared of old to me, saying:
'Yes, I have loved you with an everlasting love;
Therefore with lovingkindness I have drawn you.
Again I will build you, and you shall be rebuilt,
O virgin of Israel!
You shall again be adorned with your tambourines,
And shall go forth in the dances of those who rejoice.'"
(Jeremiah 31:3, 4)

What a sweet time in the presence of Jesus today! I want to bring forth this one truth that I found in the Book of Jeremiah —

The Scripture speaks of God's restoration work over Israel. If you remember, the Prophet Jeremiah saw the judgment of God coming upon His own people; it was God's rod of correction upon them for all the idolatry committed.

If there is one thing about knowing the Lord, it is that He is a father to us. He will correct us and coach us in the way we should be walking. He does put up with a lot, but when He finally decides to make a move, He makes it!

Again, I Will Rebuild You!

It is always the intent of the Lord to have a people who love Him for who He is, not so much for what He can do for us! He brings us up in righteousness and expects us to do what is pleasing to Him. This is how other nations or peoples see the difference in us. Our testimony is what speaks louder than anything.

Does God get angry when we disobey? I think He does not appreciate it when we follow our own desires or other gods. I also believe that when He gets upset or wrathful against us, is not His full wrath but rather only enough to get our attention.

Now the Lord will allow certain judgments to fall upon us; this judgment is calculated. Every form of discipline comes with measure! He will not destroy us but will make us feel like we have been destroyed.

It is out of this brokenness that God begins to draw us to Himself.

Though the struggle, pain or hurt comes, it will only sting for a while. For the Lord Himself will come and heal us— then restore us. He never leaves us bleeding and dying on the way. He is our loving Father and only has intentions of making us more like His Son Jesus!

Adorned Tambourines and Dance!

The time will come when the correction and the discipline will pass. Yes, the time for all your tears to dry up will take place and humility will flow out of us like a river. It is at this time that God will begin to call us to adorn our tambourines, meaning a literal season of preparation for a big celebration is on its way— so, we must get ready to celebrate and dance with joy before the Lord!

Under His Shadow Prayer

Thank you, Holy Spirit, for this wonderful promise. I know that at times the discipline seems long, and correction seems to be unending. Yet, You say in Your word, that You will break us down first and then restore us! Your hand will be mighty upon us as you complete the work you began in us. Sometimes Your hands are gentle, other times, a bit harsh. Yet in the end, You will do what is best for us. Help me to trust You my God, with the whole process, not just with half of it! Amen.

Day 6

God's Eternal Cord!

"Thus says the Lord:
Refrain your voice from weeping,
And your eyes from tears;
For your work shall be rewarded, says the Lord,
And they shall come back from the land of the enemy.
There is hope in your future, says the Lord,
That your children shall come back to their own border."
(Jeremiah 31:16-17)

One thing I have noticed about spiritual matters is that when my spirit is hungry to meet God, the heavens open— otherwise, it is just good reading.

This morning, God was gracious to me one more time and opened my eyes to this wonderful hidden truth. Let me share a bit of it with you:

You know how the Lord had brought judgment on His people for all the idolatry they had committed? He also decided that He would handle their discipline— well, along with that discipline, the Lord also provided the end of the story— a great release!

It was God's design to bring His people to a state of attention and produce brokenness in them by using the Babylonian government to bring them under captivity for 70 years. He would eventually bring them back to their homeland. You must understand that all this was done by God's design— and by the way, yes, He is the ruler of the nations!

As I meditated upon this piece of history, I came across this part of Scripture in Jeremiah 31. It's almost as if God was saying, Yes, it's going to be painful; it will hurt you a lot, and yes, this discipline will set you on fire again. Not only will your heart be aligned with Me again, but you will return to the land of your father's!

How do we know this? Well, listen to these words, "There is hope in your future, says the Lord, that your children shall come back to their own border."

In this Scripture, the Lord through Jeremiah the Prophet says, "There is hope in your future."

What the word hope means in its original language is cord. In other words, there are grounds for feeling hopeful about the future. This is really what Jeremiah is prophesying.

Let me explain further.

It is almost seeming as if the Lord in essence is saying, Look, you belong to Me and always will. Now, there is a need for me to discipline you for your wayward ways. I love you so much that I need to correct you — I don't want to lose you! Though I send you away to be under the yoke of captivity in Babylon, there is a cord from my heart to yours that will never be broken. You will never be alone, though you may feel like it! Only know that when the time of your discipline and correction is completed, I will pull you back to my heart using that same cord!

To better understand the process of God's discipline, we must know that all forms of discipline are nothing more than an arrangement of God's love towards us - whether we feel it or not! Rest in this.

Under His Shadow Prayer

Jesus, I want to thank you for this eternal cord between us.

I know that You never will allow me to fall away from your heart. Thank you for correcting my ways and teaching me your heart in life's matters. I love you so much this morning for your words, it is truly a light to my path and a lamp to my feet! Amen.

Day 7

Know & Understand the Season You Are In!

"...though you fight with the Chaldeans, you shall not succeed..." (Jeremiah 32:5)

As I opened God's word this morning, I came to this passage which I have been meditating on for a while now. History has a strange way of repeating itself; I don't understand why it is that God keeps replaying the same ideas and concepts of His will repeatedly, but I know that God has the best intentions for you and me.

In the history of Judah, King Zedekiah was the king. By this time, Babylon (the Chaldeans) had already started taking God's people into captivity and things just didn't look good for Judah. Also, at this specific time, the Prophet Jeremiah, had been thrown into prison for prophesying God's words to King Zedekiah.

You see, King Zedekiah was trying to be a leader to His people and was hearing all kinds of advice from his administration and even the so-called prophets of the Lord. I mean, it is wisdom to get counsel from others when you are facing difficulty. Now, the only problem was that there were so-called prophets of the Lord giving Zedekiah false prophetic words. They kept telling Zedekiah that things were going to get better very soon— which was a lie. Things were not going to get better any time soon.

You see, God was doing a deep work in Israel and Judah— and the prophets didn't want to say the truth for fear of the king perhaps; or maybe because they would become unpopular and not be in the good graces of the king. Whatever the reasoning, something moved these prophets to lie to the king!

Well, Jeremiah the Prophet, told it the way it was, and the king promoted him - to a dungeon! Jeremiah in essence was saying, You need to stay put and allow God to do His thing! The king didn't take those words well and shut him in a prison.

What we can learn from this wonderful revelation is that there are seasons when God needs us to be shut in with Him in the secret place. If we don't acknowledge our need for more of God, simply because we are too busy, don't worry, God will park us somehow!

Sometimes, the Lord will provide a desert experience.Yes, a place where we can be alone and hear His voice. Only through this method, will we be receptive enough to hear direction for the new season in our lives.

Remember: God is going somewhere with our life— let us be discerning and not get in the way of all that God is trying to accomplish in us.

Under His Shadow Prayer

King Jesus, I come before You with a broken and contrite spirit. I understand that the seasons in my life are set in motion by Your will. You have called me to walk in Your seasons, not mine. I surrender all this morning. Don't allow me to become anxious, desperate, and continue in my selfishness. Teach me to be patient and cause my spirit to discern the seasons of change. I love you Jesus! Amen.

Day 8

Why Does God Allow Calamities In My Life?

"You have given them this land, of which You swore to their fathers to give them—'a land flowing with milk and honey.'
And they came in and took possession of it, but they have not obeyed Your voice or walked in Your law. They have done nothing of all that You commanded them to do; therefore You have caused all this calamity to come upon them." (Jeremiah 32:22-23)

Situations in our lives don't just appear for no reason. Though some tests might come to build our faith, adversity in our lives might just be due to our lives being out of sync or alignment with God's will or divine purposes.

God has a special way of bringing us into alignment through various means. Sometimes the test might be easy, sometimes it might be hard to overcome, and there will be times where the test will almost be impossible to cross without the Lord's help! Have you ever experienced some of these tests in your life?

In the case of Judah, yes, God gave them a promise— if they would walk with God they would inherit a land that flows with milk and honey. God wasn't lying to them and so He kept His promise and gave them the land to possess.

There is something of great testing that happens to us when we get what we pray for — it's the challenge to stay passionate and focused on the Lord's agenda. To keep the fire burning till the race is finally over.

Too often, we get our miracle, our breakthrough, etc., and we quickly turn our back on the Lord's plan. Once we get what we prayed for and replenish our needs, we quickly cool off until the next crisis hits us.

Did Not Obey the Voice of God!

Once Judah took the land, their ears went deaf towards the Lord — not literally, but spiritually. They no longer wanted to hear God's commands, they no longer wanted to follow God's plan, they no longer wanted to please Him with their lives!

Isn't it always the case that when we stop listening to God's voice all hell breaks loose in our lives? Why haven't we learned from history this one great lesson? Do you understand what I am referring to? Too many cases bear this fact: We get what we want, then we shun Him away by not listening to His voice anymore.

What is God to Do?

I don't think God is playing a game with us. He knows how frail and weak we are as human beings. He knows how dependent upon His grace we need to be to survive. So, He lets us go on our own strength and wisdom until we run out of steam. It is here, where God waits patiently for us to recognize our error— then He steps in.

Calamity has only one purpose to accomplish: To bring us back to His feet, enter into repentance and worship!

Under His Shadow Prayer

My Lord, this morning I want to acknowledge Your sovereign ways. I know that You are quick to hear our prayers and answer them in Your timing. I know that when You answer, my responsibility is to acknowledge You as the giver of all things.

My posture should always be one of recognizing You as the King of my life in all things. Whether You answer my prayer or not — You still remain the One and Only King of my life. Amen.

Day 9

Learn to Refresh Others!

"I thank my God, making mention of you always in my prayers, hearing of your love and faith which you have toward the Lord Jesus and toward all the saints, that the sharing of your faith may become effective by the acknowledgment of every good thing which is in you in Christ Jesus. For we have great joy and consolation in your love, because the hearts of the saints have been refreshed by you, brother." (Philemon 4-7)

Let me say something as I feel the Spirit of the Lord upon me today: To the degree that we as God's servants are experiencing refreshing in the Spirit, is to the degree that we will be able to refresh others with His love!

Philemon was one of God's soldiers in the faith. He was not ashamed in testifying about His faith in Christ and demonstrating such powerful love to those around him. Paul acknowledged these qualities upon this godly servant.

Are the people around my life or your life, being refreshed every time we come around or they come around us? Is an impact for Christ being felt? Are they being refreshed in their lives by the words and actions you demonstrate? This subject, in my humble opinion, is huge!

If people come around us, whether in private or public, and they chit-chat even if it's for five or ten minutes, are we causing an impact? Are they happy they stopped to say, Thanks for those words! Or do they leave in regret saying, This guy is always negative and leaves me feeling downcast!

How Do We Become Refreshed in God?

1. The best way to get spiritually refreshed in God is through personal prayer. Spending some quality time daily with God will increase your faith and strengthen your inner-being. You will become a fountain of life for others by doing this.

There are so many people walking around in the Christian church without living water. Their established way of living out their Christian faith is not cutting it, they need what you have — rivers of life!

2. Reading God's Word. By reading God's word and learning

to hear God's words, will also release a healing effect upon us. It will cleanse us and renew our thinking.

3. Walking-out God's commands will instill in us spiritual authority and spiritual power. We will then be able to share His truths with power and conviction to others.

Whatever your preference of time to do these spiritual exercises is up to you. Just do them and be refreshed in His river for the sake of your own life and that of others!

Under His Shadow Prayer

Holy Spirit, bring these exercises to mind every single day. I long to be refreshed in Your river. I don't want to live an empty Christian life. I don't want to just go through the emotions of this religion. I need power, I need spiritual authority, and I need a fresh anointing upon me daily! Amen.

Day 10

Do You Believe in the Impossible?

"And again He entered Capernaum after some days, and it was heard that He was in the house. Immediately many gathered together, so that there was no longer room to receive them, not even near the door. And He preached the word to them. Then they came to Him, bringing a paralytic who was carried by four men. And when they could not come near Him because of the crowd, they uncovered the roof where He was. So when they had broken through, they let down the bed on which the paralytic was lying. When Jesus saw their faith, He said to the paralytic, 'Son, your sins are forgiven you.'" (Mark 2:1-5)

Have you ever wondered how many people need to be present for God to do miracles? Have you ever asked yourself if being in a cell group meeting versus being in a church congregation meeting would hinder God from flowing? I think not.

While meditating early this morning, the Holy Spirit brought to my attention the story of the four men who carried a paralytic to a house where Jesus was present. It was here where Christ was preaching and healing the sick.

Apparently, these four men heard that Christ was there and needed to take this particular man to the meeting. As they got to the house, they noticed it was full of people, and they couldn't get in the conventional way, so they took him up on the roof and then made a hole in the roof and lowered Him right where Jesus was speaking.

What does this say to the tenacity of these men? What does this say of people who have the faith of God to believe in the impossible?

I do believe that this is one of the things that moves the heart of God — when His creation responds to His invitation in faith. When we hear God speaking and we respond to His call, by the very act that we take steps forward in faith, God is glorified and honored by us.

So to close this devotion, it is not how big the attendance in the meeting is, it is not the place where it is being held, whether a town hall, a church, under a tree or in a house—

no, the key is: how great is the faith of God in us? Do we believe in our heart of hearts, that God can do the impossible? Let our actions speak then!

Under His Shadow Prayer

Lord Jesus, this morning I want to put my life in Your hands. I know that sometimes when I look out, things don't look too good, not too promising, and even bleak at times. I want to repent of my doubtful attitude. Forgive me. I now realize that You are not boxed-in by my perspective or my opinion. I also learn that if I have the faith of God, I will see the glory of God in any place and at any time. Amen.

Day 11

Welcome to the Inaccessible!

"Moreover the word of the Lord came to Jeremiah a second time, while he was still shut up in the court of the prison, saying, 'Thus says the Lord who made it, the Lord who formed it to establish it (the Lord is His name): Call to Me, and I will answer you, and show you great and mighty things, which you do not know.'" (Jeremiah 33:1-3)

I know that sometimes we think life is not fair, and we question why things happen to us and not others, especially our enemies, etc. Yet, for those who walk with God, things are very different. For one, we are part of an army that marches to the beat of a different drummer. We don't go with the flow of society. We flow with the heartbeat of God!

So, as we live our lives in God, we will experience things that the world has no clue about. For example, to be first, you must be last. To go up you must go down first; humility is the key to greatness and instead of hating an enemy, we are called to pray for them.

In the matter of testing, trials, or adversity, the Lord will choose to do things a bit different with us than with those who are yet to come into the knowledge of Christ. I am sure you have already figured this out if you have been walking with Christ for some time.

Under Discipline

Our lives, though free from the life of sin, are still under the subjection of the Spirit of God. It is the Spirit that knows that mind of God, so He leads us according to God's wishes. Now, God knows our lives and understands us better than we do ourselves.

Sometimes people praise us and give us recognitions which in turn create a reputation that we did not go looking for. People often think Christians are perfect people— they are not, people just assumed that they are!

One of the greatest benefits of being a believer under subjection to the Holy Spirit is that the Spirit leads us into places we thought we didn't need. See, the Spirit of God knows our inward parts, mainly our heart and mind. He knows our human tendencies and is determined to transform us by the things we will suffer.

Stuck in Prison!

It was in prison that God opened Jeremiah's vision, the ability to see beyond the prison cell. It will always be God through His Spirit releasing fresh vision to us in the darkest of places.

It is here where the Lord told Jeremiah to call upon Him for the Lord wanted to reveal to Jeremiah great and mighty things, which he did not know. What an invitation.

It is interesting that God knew exactly Jeremiah's heart regarding His time in prison. God came to visit the prophet there— right at the place and time Jeremiah needed Him.

When the Lord comes, He comes to unveil and put our hearts at peace. There are a lot of things we don't understand about what we are facing. There are many things we think we know, but we really don't! This is where God comes to unveil.

He tells Jeremiah to call Him. He is longing to reveal to Him inaccessible things, which Jeremiah had no clue about;

things that would set Jeremiah at rest and positioned Him to trust and move forward in His calling.

There are things that God will only reveal during times of distress and brokenness. These things have been set apart for those who walk in a broken and contrite spirit.

Under His Shadow Prayer

This morning my heart has been challenged one more time by Your Spirit oh God. I want the posture of my heart to always be one of yielded ness and willingness to hear and obey everything You desire of me. I don't want to live for myself or for anyone else — if it is not first for You! Amen.

Day 12

Downloads of Revelation!

"God, who at various times and in various ways spoke in time past to the fathers by the prophets, has in these last days spoken to us by His Son . . . " (Hebrews 1:1, 2)

Interesting stuff this morning! The Scripture says that God spoke to our forefathers at various times and in various ways through prophets but now speaks to us through His Son in these last days.

If you have read to any extent the books of the Old Testament, you will discover one story after another as to how God spoke to His people. Whether it was face to face in audible fashion, or through an angel, a burning bush, or directly to their hearts and minds, God revealed His will to them.

What seems very interesting to me is that God speaks to us through His Son Jesus. If this is true, then we should be listening to every word that comes forth from the mouth of Jesus, plus the letters left by revelation to all the other disciples which came directly by inspiration of the Holy Spirit.

Now unto Jesus speaking to us—

Everything Jesus shares with us is always regarding us in relation to His kingdom and the progression of this venture upon the earth. He has called us to go into all the world and to make disciples of them. The call is to teach them all He taught us.

Reading the words of Christ in the Bible is one way to discover what we should be doing for Him; it lays out our agenda in the simplest form. He will speak to us and pierce our conscience with His divine order. This is God's way.

Now, the Holy Spirit, also will take the words of Christ and embed them in our spirit. He will reveal Christ to us in deeper ways. We, by the Spirit of God, will hear what is being said between the lines-in other words, what Jesus meant to say but didn't. We have been left to unveil it through His Spirit. Only those who have ears to hear will hear these words.

As God speaks, we are left with an opportunity to run with his information and share it with unsaved friends, saved friends, in church or out of church, at a pulpit, a home cell group, or at work. These words are full of the life of God.

Yes, God is speaking these days through His Son. Are we listening to His downloads of revelation?

Under His Shadow Prayer

I know Jesus that You long to speak to Your people. I know that Your heart is that we would write all these revelations in our hearts. You created us for impact — to have an impact among those who surround us. Please lead by Your Spirit and cause me to always hear Your words. I long to be more susceptible to Your voice. I want to hear Your voice. Lastly, help me to walk it out daily. Don't allow me to be only a hearer of Your word, but a doer as well! Amen.

Day 13

Going a Little Farther!

"Then Jesus came with them to a place called Gethsemane, and said to the disciples, 'Sit here while I go and pray over there.' And He took with Him Peter and the two sons of Zebedee, and He began to be sorrowful and deeply distressed. Then He said to them, 'My soul is exceedingly sorrowful, even to death. Stay here and watch with Me.' He went a little farther and fell on His face, and prayed, saying, 'O My Father, if it is possible, let this cup pass from Me; nevertheless, not as I will, but as You will.'" (Matthew 29:36-39)

I can appreciate the corporate prayer settings, and they do have their place in the body of Christ. I believe in coming together to declare what God is saying in a corporate sense and the prayers of agreement— all this is great stuff!

As good as corporate prayer is, there is a type of prayer that cannot be substituted; this type of prayer cannot be done without the mind and the heart being engaged, and it cannot be done hastily.

The type of prayer that I am referring to is the personal prayer that allows God to show the recipient a deeper sense of life and holiness. It teaches the man and woman who will dare to believe what God truly thinks and knows about them. It's a prayer time where people of God fall prostrate before God and allow Him to perform His work in them. It is just like a doctor performing surgery on a patient. It might be painful, but it will always be worth it!

As much as Jesus valued John, James, and Peter; and as much as He desired to teach them about a deeper life in God, He had one thing that was more important than teaching them in view, it was to meet the heavenly Father for Himself.

"He went a little farther and fell on His face, and prayed, saying, 'O My Father, if it is possible, let this cup pass from Me; nevertheless, not as I will, but as You will.'"

Most believers will only go as far as they need to. They will only pray until it starts to cost them something; they will only fast until it gets hard for their flesh to deal with having no food; they will only give offerings until it starts to hurt them. Yet, during all these games that Christians play there are always people who will go a little further.

The need to touch God has never been greater; the need to be full of God's fire has never been greater; and the need to go a little further, has never been greater!

Under His Shadow Prayer

King Jesus, I am Your servant and I am hearing Your heart this morning. I get it! It is not enough to just read the Bible and say a little prayer; it is not enough to fast till noon and hope that our ritual was enough to move a mountain or two. These times demand extraordinary praying, fasting, and sacrifice. Jesus, help me to go a little further! Amen.

Day 14

A Word from the Lord!

"When Jeremiah entered the dungeon and the cells, and Jeremiah had remained there many days, then Zedekiah the king sent and took him out. The king asked him secretly in his house, and said, 'Is there any word from the Lord?'" (Jeremiah 37:16, 17)

As I pondered this verse during my quiet time today, I came across the idea that it really doesn't matter who you are, or who you think you are— sooner or later, you will need a word from the Lord for your life.

I believe that people who are conscious of God, will always look for the opinion of God and make the effort to find out what God thinks of certain matters involving their own lives. Now King Zedekiah had fallen from the favor of the Lord and had mistreated the prophet Jeremiah in the past, but he was now in need of a word from the Lord. Why didn't King Zedekiah go back to the pillow prophets (pillow prophets are false prophets who prophesy fleshly ideas or half-truths that tickle people's ears, but don't bring conviction to the heart to awaken the dead spiritual condition of God's people) who were already prophesying lies to the people? At first when the the Prophet Jeremiah gave instruction and prophesied to Zedekiah, he was disdained and abused by those in the king's administration. Why then was Zedekiah begging Jeremiah for a word from the Lord, if he truly didn't want to hear the truth?

Let me tell you why.

You see, the truth of God cuts deep. It convicts the human heart to its very core. Anyone who speaks or prophesies God's truth will always make an impact! Truth will leave a mark wherever it lands. No one can hear the truth and walk away pretending they didn't hear it — the truth never goes away! Zedekiah was under the spell of God's truth.

So, when things truly matter, when things are down and out and a word from the Lord is truly needed, God has His people ready to speak.

I think that we as believers should always make every effort to be a people who seek God for His counsel, for a word from heaven, before acting on anything. When you become a person who seeks the face of God, people around you will know it!

Trust me, if you carry the prophetic word upon you and it's in you— people will find you, even if they don't like you, or appreciate you! They will come to you like Zedekiah did with Jeremiah, and say, Is there any word from the Lord?

Under His Shadow Prayer

Heavenly Father, I come to you today with the desire to seek Your face and find out Your thoughts on matters concerning my life and ministry. I know that only You have true wisdom and as the Apostle Peter said, "Where do we go Lord, if only You have words of life?" As I prostrate my heart before You, will You speak to me? Will you align my life and purpose with Yours? Give me a word from Your heart oh God! Amen.

Day 15

It Was Fitting!

"For it was fitting for Him, for whom are all things and by whom are all things, in bringing many sons to glory, to make the captain of their salvation perfect through sufferings." (Hebrews 2:10)

Christ has been perfected through sufferings. What a way to be perfected! I believe that as we walk with God daily, much of what we will face, in the sense of opposition, will serve us as character training and development.

As I have been pondering this portion of Scripture, there are things that I don't know how to unfold, being that the heart of God was to bring His creation back to their original purpose and intent, the ways of God seem so different than mine.

It Was Fitting!

First, the Father thought it fitting for Christ to go through all

He went through. This doesn't make sense to anyone who is bound to their selfish ways. There is no way to understand this lifestyle if one is not willing to die to self and embrace God's purpose.

For us who believe, the cross of Christ is key! We can't follow Jesus if we don't die to self. It is not just hard but also impossible. The selfish carnal nature within us, must suffer a deadly blow before God can flow through us and bring us to a higher ground.

It was impossible for Christ to walk out this life for God if He didn't die to His own dreams. It would not have been possible if Jesus had stayed stilling in glory and reigning from above. No sir!

As a matter of fact, Christ's dream involved lost humanity. The only way to gain access to our hearts was if He would come down to our level and suffer the humility and shame of an earthly life.

I thank the Father He sent Jesus— He was rewarded for His obedience.

A Name Above Every Name!

"Let this mind be in you which was also in Christ Jesus, who, being in the form of God, did not consider it robbery to be equal with God, but made Himself of no reputation, taking the form of a bondservant, and coming in the likeness of men. And being found in appearance as a man, He humbled Himself and became obedient to the point of death, even the death of the cross. Therefore, God also has highly exalted Him and given Him the name, which is above every name, that at the name of Jesus every knee should bow, of those in heaven, and of those on earth, and of those under the earth, and that every tongue should confess that Jesus Christ is Lord, to the glory of God the Father." (Philippians 2:5-11)

Because Christ died first, He now lives forever!

Under His Shadow Prayer

It is my heart's desire to be like You Jesus. I want to follow in Your footsteps every single day of my life. I don't want my own will, I want Yours! Help me to please you with all that is within me! Amen.

Day 16

The Ministry of Life in Living Color!

"For in that He Himself has suffered, being tempted, He is able to aid those who are tempted." (Hebrews 2:18)

"Blessed be the God and Father of our Lord Jesus Christ, the Father of mercies and God of all comfort, who comforts us in all our affliction so that we will be able to comfort those who are in any affliction with the comfort with which we ourselves are comforted by God." (2 Corinthians 1:3-5)

When I look deeper into the lives of those who have caused the greatest impact for Jesus, I can't help seeing the many afflictions and troubles they confronted while walking with God.

Some of the adversities that came upon them were due to people who were against them for reasons that really didn't make sense. For example, why would anyone want to kill the Apostle Paul for the simple reason of helping others find the truth in Jesus? Why would anyone want to crucify Christ when He never committed any wrongdoing against anyone? It just doesn't make sense. So, we are left with only one reason for such adversity— the forces of evil opposing the power of the gospel.

Whatever the adversity was that came upon these servants, God used it for His own good. It was of such magnitude that these servants of God were found seeking God for strength and for encouragement. Yes, all this God used and not only to mold and shape them but to teach them to find comfort in God!

What does this say about you and me? It says that we ourselves will face many adversities to test and try us. There are many areas that you and I must be tested in— God will not leave any stones unturned.

The Ministry of Life!

The ministry of life is simply this: God will allow adversity to hit us hard; it will break us and God Himself then will pick up our cause and strengthen us and rebuild us. After we have experienced His glory, He will use us to share that same experience with those who are hurting. Whatever flows from us is called the ministry of life.

Whenever we minister out of an experience that we have come through, we pour on others the mercy and compassion of God. Others will feel the love and nourishing heart of the Father coming forth through us.

Under His Shadow Prayer

Lord Jesus, I want to first thank You for my life. You gave me this life with the intent that I would live for You and please You with it. To live for myself wouldn't be Your design and to live for other reasons outside of Your will, would be a sure recipe for corruption and destruction. Also, Lord, I want to thank You for all the opportunities You have presented for me to grow and develop as one of Your servants. Though the tests seem difficult and unending, Your grace continues to flow and to fill my broken nature. Thank You King Jesus, I love You and need you more than ever! Amen.

Day 17

Vision of Man in Captivity!

"So now, I will break his yoke bar from upon you, and I will tear off your shackles." (Nahum 1:3)

If there is something about Christianity that other world religions don't promote, it is the power of the blood of Jesus.

It is the blood of Jesus that breaks every chain known to mankind. It frees our conscience, it frees our mindsets, it removes our guilty stains of sin, it heals our physical body, and it empowers us for the future spiritual battles! Thank You Jesus for the blood!

As I spent time in prayer this morning at our intercessory prayer meeting, the Lord came to me with an astounding vision. I want to share this with you for I know that God has given it for a reason:

I saw an individual handcuffed and on his knees. As I looked closer, the man looked like he was deformed in his legs and truly in a bad posture. I really couldn't tell why he was in that position, but apparently in the vision, it was understood that he had been placed in the posture by someone else. It seemed like someone had bound him hand and foot, and he was unable to free himself. Suddenly the scene changed, and I saw the same man outside this room walking and fully healed! I thought to myself, did I miss something? How was he healed? How did it happen? I want to know! It was here that I asked the Lord, Lord, how did this man end up well and walking outside, being that he was in bad shape and bound?

The Lord opened my eyes and I saw how this healing took place. Check this out: As the man was on his knees and broken, his hands bound, and no way out to escape, a voice came from heaven and spoke to him. This voice said, Get up! You are healed.

The man couldn't do it. The voice kept repeating, Get up! You are healed.

Finally, the man reached deep into his very core for strength—then he stood on his feet and unshackled his hands. End of Vision.

What I Learned from this Vision

There are a few things that God revealed to me from this vision. First, God showed me that the prophetic word for healing is given from above and it is to be spiritually discerned and applied. Secondly, once the prophetic word is given, it's up to the recipient to believe it and enter it. In other words, when instruction is given, we need to walk it out even though we may not feel anything different. We keep walking towards what God said (symbolized by the vision where the man drew strength from his inner core). The healing will take place as we walk in the instruction that God has given. If no instruction is given, then nothing will happen. If instruction from the Lord is given, then His word is as good as receiving our healing!

Under His Shadow Prayer

Jesus, teach me to hear Your voice for my life. It doesn't matter the situation, Your word is more powerful than anything created. Help me to hear Your instructions and give me the faith to enter it. Help me to walk in a supernatural dimension. Amen.

Day 18

Today, If You Hear His Voice!

"Therefore, as the Holy Spirit says:
'Today, if you will hear His voice,
Do not harden your hearts as in the rebellion,
In the day of trial in the wilderness,
Where your fathers tested Me, tried Me...'" (Hebrews 3:7-9)

In reading and meditating upon these verses, I felt that the Lord truly wants to bring us into a place of blessing. It is His intent to enrich our lives in every way.

Now, too often, we don't see God's intentions, wishes or desires. We tend to see only the negative side of things.

In seeing the blessing of God way in the distance, we also see the present. In the present we must deal with a slavery mindset. Remember, the Hebrew children were enslaved for over 400 years. Is it any wonder that they had a hard time adjusting to ways of God and their understanding of hearing God's voice?

One thing we as followers of Christ must keep before us, is the fact that God will always test our lives with the purpose of reformatting our mindset. Reformatting our minds is key for it prepares us for what God has in store for us.

The testing of God is not just done because God is mad or wants to give us a hard time living our lives out; no sir, every test has the intention of getting us to a place where we see ourselves the way God sees us. When we see our true self in the light of His presence, we will make the changes necessary.

Today, If . . .

Every day that the children of Israel woke up, they had an opportunity to hear God's message and direction. Every morning was full of new mercy and opportunity to please God, but would they?

Apparently, the children of Israel, were more interested in their own needs than what God had on His agenda and thus rebelled continually. This is all too common for God's children to do. We must always guard ourselves from ourselves (and our earthly nature).

All this rebellion eventually consumed their hearts. They hardened their hearts against God and that was enough to cancel or abort their futures. The rebellion got to the level where God said in His own heart, If that is what they want, then they can have it. I will not be part of any of that idolatry and selfishness.

The Scripture says that He gave them over to their lusts. Isn't this a scary place to be? No God to defend you, no consciousness of His presence to hold you back, it was not a good place.

In closing, always remember that if today, you hear His voice, don't harden your heart!

Under His Shadow Prayer

Holy Spirit, please guide me today in all my ways. Make me so sensitive to Your voice and help me respond quickly to it. I don't want to miss out on anything you might have in store for me. Also, guard my heart from secret sin or presumptuous sin. Keep everything in me in Your light! Amen.

Day 19

God, Help Me Enter Into Your Dreams!

"And to whom did He swear that they would not enter His rest, but to those who did not obey? So we see that they could not enter in because of unbelief." (Hebrews 3:18, 19)

Pondering the heart of the matter regarding the Hebrew children, has made me consider in a deeper way the high price of rebellion. To abort an idea that comes from the Lord, simply because we just can't see what God sees is really no excuse!

Too often we have canceled God's best for us. We have embraced the urgent instead of the important! We have convinced ourselves that the way we perceive life to be is the way it really is. No wonder the Scripture rightly says, **"There is a way which seems right to a man and appears straight before him, but its end is the way of death."** (Proverbs 14:12) – Amplified Bible.

The only One with the right plan here, is the creator of the universe.

When God speaks to our spirit and lays out a special plan for us, a plan that will guarantee success. Why is it that our flesh quickly opposes what God says and attacks our minds and hearts with the old nature(which by the way, has nothing in store for us, but corruption and disgrace)?

This morning's revelation has to do with the consequence of not obeying the Lord. Is it only disobedience or is there another motive behind our actions? I believe there is a very powerful force at work— a force so strong that it will not allow the servant of God to cross over — it is called unbelief.

Entering Rest!

Why is it that too many believers find themselves pursuing or chasing dreams, instead of following the dreams chasing them? You see, when God speaks to our hearts, it guarantees a tranquil state of mind. When God leads us towards anything, there is a peace that surpasses our understanding. When it is not God leading but our own selfish ideas, then we face this uphill climb that has no end! At the end of our pursuit, we still don't have rest or peace.

Now, the man or woman of God, who sets their heart on pleasing the Father, will always be honored, and favored. Why is this? Well, my experience has been that when we don't walk in unbelief, we are able to see what God has in view for us. Knowing that God is pleased with our pursuit of what He wishes and desires for us brings about a peace like no other.

We can pursue many things in life, but only a few things are worth pursuing — this would be God things! Learn to listen to His voice for what is exactly on His agenda for you! The secret truly lies in knowing what is of the Lord and what is birthed in our carnal minds.

Under His Shadow Prayer

King Jesus — You are still the King of my life! There is no other God like who has my best interests at heart! I love You for being my Guide in this short life. I truly want my aspirations to be birthed by Your spirit in me. Don't allow me to pursue empty dreams. Holy Spirit keep me in check now and always. Amen.

Day 20

His Way and How to Walk It Out!

"Now all the captains of the forces, Johanan the son of Kareah, Jezaniah the son of Hoshaiah, and all the people, from the least to the greatest, came near and said to Jeremiah the prophet, 'Please, let our petition be acceptable to you, and pray for us to the Lord your God, for all this remnant (since we are left but a few of many, as you can see), that the Lord your God may show us the way in which we should walk and the thing we should do.'" (Jeremiah 42:1-3)

There are several ways that a servant of the Lord decides to please God with his life. Some decide to follow God by chance, others follow God by being led by other people, and some desire to know God's ways and follow those steps. I have discovered that those who position themselves to follow God's way by firsthand revelation are the ones who usually become God's leaders.

In our story above, God's people needed spiritual leadership; they needed to know what to do with their futures, so they spoke to Jeremiah the Prophet.

This remnant that was left back in Judah needed direction from God and the only person who knew anything about God's divine order or God's will was apparently Jeremiah the Prophet.

Notice their prayer request:

"Please, let our petition be acceptable to you, and pray for us to the Lord your God, for all this remnant (since we are left but a few of many, as you can see), that the Lord your God may show us the way in which we should walk and the thing we should do."

These servants of God were not looking for anything that had to do with materialism or convenience; I believe that these servants had outgrown these things and were now ready to truly find out what God had in mind. They seemed to be more interested in two major things: the way in which they should walk, and knowing what they should do.

Knowing where to go and knowing how to get there are perhaps some of the most valuable elements for the servant who desires to please the Lord.

As you walk with God, ask yourself these two questions continually—Where am I going? How should I get there? I have found that this is the most satisfying way to live out this life.

Under His Shadow Prayer

Precious Jesus, my Lord — this morning I long for Your heart and will for my life. I don't want to do my own thing — I want Your thing! I need my life to be surrounded by Your favor and the only way this will happen, is, if I walk under Your direction and in the path, you outline for me. Once I find this direction, I know You will teach me the details on how to walk it out. I love You with all my heart this morning Jesus. Thank You for Your Word and Spirit. Amen.

Day 21

Pierced By His Word!

"For the word of God is living and powerful, and sharper than any two-edged sword, piercing even to the division of soul and spirit, and of joints and marrow, and is a discerner of the thoughts and intents of the heart. And there is no creature hidden from His sight, but all things are naked and open to the eyes of Him to whom we must give account." (Hebrews 4:12, 13)

As I meditated upon this portion of Scripture, once again the Spirit of the Lord quickened my mind and heart to realize the great value of God's words spoken to our inner being. Nothing quickens our spirit and soul like the very words of God piercing through. Whether a man may be dead, lukewarm, or alive in God, the words given by inspiration of the Holy Spirit — will revolutionize anyone who lends a spiritual ear to them.

The word of God pierces, divides, and discerns the intentions of the heart.

Let us look at it:

The very words of God have a piercing effect. With their double edged capability, they can cut right through any fixed mindset. If you have any preconceived ideas, it would be best to check them in at the door. They will be shredded to pieces!

Along with the effect of piercing, God's word will also divide the soul and spirit. What this means is that God's word will divide that which is from the Lord and that which is birthed in the womb of the flesh, birthed in self. Only the word of God can have this effect. Isn't this interesting?

One can show up with some idea and as one reads and meditates upon God's word, it quickens the heart that is given to selfishness. It exposes it and the servant of God is left with a decision to make. This is how this works.

The word will quickly unveil all that did not come from God! Finally, the word of God will discern the thoughts and intents of the heart. What does this mean? Well, it means that whatever thoughts you have had, and all secret intentions that are hidden in the corridors of the heart, will be exposed before the light of God's words.

We might be able to fool some people with our fancy ideas, but not God. We might be able to pull the wool over some people's eyes using our fancy words, but not God. The Holy Spirit will use the word of God to unveil and discern in your own personal life, if you are being true to truth! This will always be God's way.

Under His Shadow Prayer

Lord, make me a lover of Your words. Help me to consume Your word every day. I need Your wisdom; I need You to continually reveal my intentions and discern my ways. It is my desire to please You with all that You have given me. I don't want to miss out on anything Oh Lord! Have mercy on me. Amen.

Day 22

Rightly Corrected!

"Do not fear, O Jacob My servant," says the Lord,
'For I am with you;
For I will make a complete end of all the nations
To which I have driven you,
But I will not make a complete end of you.
I will rightly correct you,
For I will not leave you wholly unpunished.'" (Jeremiah 46:28)

Times of meditation are so valuable when coupled with fasting and prayer; it is during these times that the Holy Spirit somehow finds the mark in our hearts and shoots with the intent to embrace our hungry hearts. Thank you, Lord, for that!

In awesome meditation this morning, the Holy Spirit caused me to see God's justice, judgment, and restoration. Yes, His mindset is not like mine. Obviously, God sees the beginning from the end.

In this portion of Scripture, Jeremiah is once again sharing God's prophetic word and relates with the people of God His very heart.

If we learn to see our life the way God sees it, we won't falter as much as we do without His perspective. One of these days, we will have to realize that there are only two roads to follow: His way or the way of the flesh.

When God wasn't happy with all the idolatry that His people were engaged in, He decided to bring judgment upon them. What seems interesting is this thought: the nations that God used to bring calamity upon His people are now being judged by God Himself! In other words, the Lord used them to do His dirty work, if you will and now, He is going to punish them for doing it. Very interesting! Listen to this: **"For I will make a complete end of all the nations to which I have driven you."**

Then He turns and looks at His own people and says the following, **"But I will not make a complete end of you. I will rightly correct you, for I will not leave you wholly unpunished."**

In other words, God is not letting anyone off the hook! The only difference is that He is making an end of those nations He used to punish His own people, but He is rightly correcting His own. They were not going to get away with anything!

You see, God loves us that much, that He won't let us get away with wrongdoing at any cost. He will take care of us in the most loving of ways! Did I say loving ways? Yes, I did. You see, His ways are only loving, they can't be any other way, for His nature is love!

Under His Shadow Prayer

Lord Jesus, I love you with all my heart this morning. Your mercy over my life has been amazing; Your grace has been more than abundant, and Your compassions are never-ending. Thank You for watching over me and taking care of my life the way You do. I may not understand everything about Your justice, love and mercy — but I will embrace You with all that is within me! Amen.

Day 23

A Time for the Sword!

"O you sword of the Lord,
How long until you are quiet?
Put yourself up into your scabbard,
Rest and be still!
How can it be quiet,
Seeing the Lord has given it a charge
Against Ashkelon and against the seashore?
There He has appointed it." (Jeremiah 47:6, 7)

In studying and meditating the season of great distress and trial in the life of the people of God, one can only just imagine how it might have felt to have the Lord, by His righteous right hand, bring judgment upon Judah.

Now, God's people had been warned by the Prophet Jeremiah one too many times. They (God's people) knew exactly how God was feeling towards them living out their lustful pleasures with other gods. Only thing is that God's people did not have any clue that all of that was coming their way.

I can just hear people cry out in despair before God, saying, Lord, why are you allowing all this to come upon us? We are sorry for our backsliding, we are so sorry for our idolatry, we are so sorry for walking away from Your laws — please forgive us!"

I don't believe God's judgment came upon His people for just a one-time offense; I think judgment was unleashed after a repeated effort from the Lord to try and make His people turn from their ways. God kept on knocking and pleading until God's dread release came!

The Sword of the Lord and the Dread Release.

There comes a time when the Lord is forced to come after us and correct us. He will do this before it is too late. I call this the dread release. He will release us into a dreadful time of correction and duress. He does all this because He is a loving God, not because He is an unkind Father!

The sword of the Lord will not be put away until it does its perfect work in us!

Here's a question of great interest: Does God eventually get tired of our foolishness, sin, and compromise? I don't believe He measures or bases His judgment on His irritation, but rather on His immense love. He knows that certain sins are destroying us, and before it gets to the point of no return — He steps in! Now this is love!

You see, when the Lord gives charge to His sword to accomplish certain work, He will allow us to go through a season of brokenness. It will not cease from its dreadful butchering until our hearts have repented and restored!

Under His Shadow Prayer

Holy Spirit, this day, I want to invite You to carry me on eagle's wings. I need to be in the season You have laid out for me. I don't want to be found in the place that I want to be, but instead in Your divine place – the place where You will get the most glory from me! Lord guide me throughout this day and allow me to see You like I have not seen You before! Amen.

Day 24

Recognizing Opportunity!

"And Elisha said to him, 'Take a bow and some arrows.'
So he took himself a bow and some arrows. Then he said to the king of Israel, 'Put your hand on the bow.'
So he put his hand on it, and Elisha put his hands on the king's hands. And he said, 'Open the east window,' and he opened it.
Then Elisha said, 'Shoot,' and he shot.
And he said, 'The arrow of the Lord's deliverance and the arrow of deliverance from Syria; for you must strike the Syrians at Aphek till you have destroyed them.'
Then he said, 'Take the arrows,' so he took them.
And he said to the king of Israel, 'Strike the ground,' so he struck three times, and stopped. And the man of God was angry with him, and said, 'You should have struck five or six times; then you would have struck Syria till you had destroyed it! But now you will strike Syria only three times.'"
(2 Kings 13:13-18)

What an amazing lesson God has shown me in this story with the prophet Elisha and the king of Israel, Joash.

God always has a plan for His people; they are never left without God's favor. Just when the enemy thought they had Israel trapped, God always made a way. This is the same God who works on our behalf — just as He was with Israel and Judah, He will be with you and me.

How Badly Do You Want Something?

When you want something badly, when you need something to take place right now, when God is offering you an opportunity to establish yourself, whether through a ministry opportunity, a promotion, or an open door that you have been looking for — one must take it and run with it. It is the Lord! The Prophet Elisha had said to King Joash that God was getting ready to deliver them from the Syrians. All King Joash had to do was follow instruction and follow his heart.

This is not hard to do, if indeed, your wishes are passionate! So, Elisha speaks to Joash and tells him to, **"Take the arrows"** and **"strike the ground."**

Joash took the arrows and struck the ground only three

times, and then stopped.

Missing an Opportunity!

"And the man of God was angry with him, and said, 'You should have struck five or six times; then you would have struck Syria till you had destroyed it! But now you will strike Syria only three times.'"

Why did King Joash stop hitting the ground after three times? Why couldn't he go more times and establish what was in his heart?

I believe God looks at our hearts' passions and desires then proceeds to give us an opportunity to manifest what we have inside our hearts. We can't afford to miss an opportunity once God opens the door for us.

The Bible says that Elisha was angry with the king. It was God's way of saying to King Joash, Had you obeyed your heart, you would have demolished the Syrians. But now you will only strike them three times.

When our hearts are on fire, we will go all out! When our hearts are not really into something, we will only strike the ground three times. By not following our passion, we will consequently not reach our full potential.

Prophetic Dream of Opportunity

As I slept last night, the Lord came to me in a dream:

I dreamt that an old friend of mine, and fellow musician, had booked a concert for our band to play. This concert was on a big stage, like a Fiesta Texas theme park or at the Washington Mall in DC. We were to do only 3 songs at the very end, for this is what my friend told me. I asked him why only 3 songs? Why not 10 songs? He couldn't explain why he only chose 3. He said, "Where are we going to get more songs in such a short time?

I said, "I will figure them out and will get them done! I'm not wasting this opportunity of a lifetime on such a big stage."

I believe that the Lord was speaking prophetically and is getting me ready for some great opportunities that are headed my way. Don't know what they are, but they are coming.

Under His Shadow Prayer

Jesus, help me to recognize the opportunities that are coming my way. I don't want to miss what you are doing in me Lord. Please Holy Spirit, will you guide me every step of the way! Amen.

Day 25

Tipped Over!

"Moab has been at ease from his youth;
He has settled on his dregs,
And has not been emptied from vessel to vessel,
Nor has he gone into captivity.
Therefore his taste remained in him,
And his scent has not changed.
'Therefore behold, the days are coming,' says the Lord,
'That I shall send him wine-workers
Who will tip him over
And empty his vessels
And break the bottles.'" (Jeremiah 48:11, 12)

Here's a principle for us to learn: Moab has been at ease from his youth!

In my seeking after the Lord this morning, this one Scripture came to my mind and heart.

The Lord points out the country of Moab (modern day Jordan). He goes on to explain how as a nation they have been at ease. I want to use this illustration to typify a certain kind of believer. A believer who has been negligent with his or her spiritual experience.

As we walk with God through life, we will always be challenged to align our hearts with God and align our whole being with His purpose and plan.

Now, the human tendency, the flesh, doesn't sympathize with this type of living and practice. As a matter of fact, it wants to do the opposite of following God. It goes the opposite way into rebellion and selfishness.

The opposite of being at ease is being attentive to the moving of the Spirit. Moving with God's Spirit takes us out of our comfort zone into God's zone. This is where we want to find ourselves daily.

From Vessel to Vessel

To the point that the prophet is making, he illustrates Moab like the making of wine. Wine is crushed first, and then it's put into vessels (bottles of skin). To get rid of all the dregs, the wine must then be moved from one bottle to another, until it becomes perfected in taste.

The issue here was that Moab always looked for the easy and convenient way to live. It didn't allow itself to be carried into captivity and by this, I mean, God wanted to test them, but they ran from God, they ran from the test. This sounds so much like modern Christians! They run away from God's dealings and buy into the foolishness of a convenient, self-absorbing, self-indulging gospel.

The consequence of not allowing God to do work in us is detrimental. Just like in wine. If the wine is not allowed to be transferred from one vessel to another, it will not have the taste it should. It will not change from bad to good, and from good to great!

Who Will Tip Him Over?

I don't think it will allow anyone to stay the same. I believe that after a while, God will use whatever means possible to do this process. The question is: Will you be ready to be changed? What will your attitude be?

Don't allow the Lord to be the One to push you into the process; learn to recognize the dealings of God with you. Get acquainted with His desires, so you don't miss out on anything He wants to do.

Under His Shadow Prayer

Lord Jesus, do as you wish with my heart. I long to follow You. I long to be broken by You. It is my desire to be changed and transformed into Your image today and the next day and the next day, etc. Please show me Your ways and help me to walk out my destiny in You! Amen.

Day 26

The Promise Keeper!

"For when God made a promise to Abraham, because He could swear by no one greater, He swore by Himself, saying, 'Surely blessing I will bless you, and multiplying I will multiply you.' And so, after he had patiently endured, he obtained the promise." (Hebrews 6:13-15)

Here's something very interesting that we see all through the nature of God— He is a promise keeping God! God never lies! When God makes a promise to you or anyone else, you can rest assured that it will come to pass.

What does a fulfilled promise look like?

This is a great question.

Many times in our life, we will face situations that are complex and hard to solve with our own wisdom or strength, so we pray for guidance, and we will pray for the Lord to give us some creative alternative way to get out from under our duress.

I believe we have all prayed these kinds of prayers.

In response to our prayer, the Holy Spirit may release a promise to us. It may come to us through His written word, through the preaching of His word, through a prophetic dream or vision, or simply through the mouth of one of the local prophets from our place of worship.

God Is Different from Us!

How the answer comes might shock us all, for the Lord works in mysterious ways. You see when we pray, we pretty much have a picture of what we need or want done. God knows this. The thing is — God also has a picture of how He needs to act and when He needs to act!

God doesn't only answer our prayer on the basis that we need or want something. He answers prayers based on everyone and everything that surrounds us. You see, everything that surrounds us will be greatly affected by the answered prayer. We must keep this in mind the next time we are waiting upon the Lord to answer one of our prayers.

As we wait upon God's promise, we must also be aware that God is also moving other things around and accommodating or restructuring people, places, and situations. That is why when God gives a promise, the mature know better than to start whining and complaining about an unanswered prayer – for much of it, depends on all that God is shifting on our behalf!

If we long to grow up and mature in the Lord, then let us learn to do what Abraham did. Listen to this: **"And so, after he had patiently endured, he obtained the promise."** There is a key to answered promises, Abraham taught us how to get there!

Under His Shadow Prayer

Dear heavenly Father, I don't want to be impatient with all that You have promised me. I don't want to complain and get all shaken up simply because my prayers are not being answered yet. I do believe that every promise You make, you cause it to manifest! Help me to wait with anticipation on all that You are going to do! Amen.

Day 27

Never Look for the Easy Way!

"Enter by the narrow gate; for wide is the gate and broad is the way that leads to destruction, and there are many who go in by it. Because narrow is the gate and difficult is the way which leads to life, and there are few who find it." (Matthew 7:13, 14)

In walking out the principles of the Lord, it is never easy to carry them out. We walk these out by pure obedience, not because we feel good doing it. Most people I know who walk with God, know that the real path of life is narrow and difficult, thus, making the uncommitted follower to quit or look for the broad gate!

Looking for the easy way to anything, has never brought any honor to anyone. Short cuts, cheating, copying others, and stepping on others to get ahead, has never paid well. One may think that they have gained an edge by finding an "easy way," but let me tell you, the end will not be good! Too many of us have already tried it, and we found out that it doesn't reward you in the long haul.

I was watching television the other day, and a several infomercials came on within 2- or 3-minute time span; you know what I am talking about - those infomercials that announce a better way to gain financial freedom, an insurance policy that really gives low premium with low deductibles, or the lose the weight and get fit in 3 days, type of thing.

Let me tell you, it all sounds very enticing – big results with very little effort, hmmm...sounds too good to be true, doesn't it?

As I watched the last infomercial on this commercial break, it was one where this woman came out and said she lost a considerable amount of weight in a very short time – this was the one that caught my attention. As I heard her speak and make her attempt to sell the product, I thought to myself, this is a bunch of bolognas!

Here's what went through my mind:

First, if you lose all that considerable amount of weight in a very short time, by using a band or pills, or some magic cream, or eating and drinking some weed from some God-forsaken town in another universe – when will the person using the product(s), learn the lesson of discipline?

The narrow path is a path of discipline! The broad road is the path of an undisciplined life. There is no magic in anything; we must discipline our lives in all areas, if we are to be successful in all areas.

Under His Shadow Prayer

King Jesus, once again, I come to You with humility in my heart. I don't want anything easy in my life. I don't want no easy road or shortcut to my success. I want to walk with You every step of the way so you may teach me the secrets to success in God! I love You my King! Amen.

Day 28

Failing Strength!

"He made my strength fail;
The Lord delivered me into the hands of those whom I am not able to withstand." (Lamentation 1:14)

When I ponder what the word of God says regarding human strength, one can only wonder what makes man think that he can do above and beyond without God? The very thought of a human being thinking that they are self-sufficient should be a sin!

One of the interesting notes here is that God will always expose our frailty. Though we might think that we will never fail, though we might conclude that certain things cannot happen to us, don't be too self-assured of this. I get all the think positive jargon, I get all the issues with the confessing with your mouth thing, but let me just say, human strength, as mighty as it might be, will never amount to God's strength!

So, to expose man's pride and arrogance, God will do a very strange thing, He will cause your strength to fail. What does this look like?

Well, let me just say that things will begin to look and feel different around you. Your accomplishments will seem sickening to you, the work of your hands will no longer be satisfying. Everything that you used to do that brought you success — will not bring success anymore! Your friends will turn against you and all the possibilities that seemed promising at one point, will self-destruct. Do you understand me now? Has this ever happened to you?

One of the characteristics of prideful and arrogant people is that they tend to overpower those that can't defend themselves. They tend to control and manipulate weaker people until the Lord decides that it's got to stop! When this happens, the Lord will bring those whom you thought they couldn't defend themselves, to overpower and out do you! You won't be able to withstand this spiritual tsunami that will come upon you.

In teaching us valuable character and life lessons, God will give us a reality check. He will allow us to go through seasons of despair so that we may be humbled and broken. Once the lesson is learned, things will begin to take a different form. It is at this place in God, that we will be able to once again be exalted by His hand!

Under His Shadow Prayer

Lord, today I need You more than ever. My sin of selfishness is ever before me. Will you look at my hard heart and deliver me from myself? I realized this morning as I spent this quality time with you, that my strength failing, is a sure sign that you are bringing me into a much-needed level of humility. Lord, it is the cry of my heart for You to teach me Your words — that I might not sin against You! Amen.

Day 29

Only through Jesus!

"...but now, once at the end of the ages, He has appeared to put away sin by the sacrifice of Himself." (Hebrews 9:26)

"For it is not possible that the blood of bulls and goats could take away sins." (Hebrews 10:4)

In my early morning devotion today, I came across these beautiful verses that confirm Christ's awesome sacrifice for us sinners! No one can ever do what Christ came to do upon the earth. He will stand alone forever and ever!

It was the Father's idea to send His only begotten Son so that everyone who believed in Him, would not perish but would enter into life with Him.

As I pondered these thoughts written in Scripture, I came to a greater understanding that it is only through Christ, that we can stand before God. There is no other name given to mankind by which we can be established in our hearts and minds. It is through the Spirit of the Lord, that we understand God's wisdom, and God's wisdom is Christ!

As good as a person that you might think you are, and as well versed in the Bible that you might think you are none of these things, have anything to do with what Christ has accomplished for us at the cross of Calvary.

Our good works, our good behavior, our good manners, are all part of being civil in society, and it has nothing to do with God! What has everything to do with God, is our understanding of who He is and what He has done for us.

You see, Christ is the perfect sacrifice offered for you and me. Without Him, we would have no sacrifice to offer, being that bulls and goats were not sufficient to cleanse us from our sins and purify us before the Father. Christ came as the perfect sacrificial Lamb and offered His life instead for us sinners!

In Times of Restoration . . .

When my heart gets cold, when my spirit is lukewarm within me, when the fire of His passion within is burnt out — where do I go for restoration? Where do I go to get my spirit back on track with God? Who do I run to when my life is cold and indifferent?

My friends, we run to Jesus, the Author and Finisher of our faith. When things get rough, lonely, difficult, challenging, etc., the only answer is Jesus, the Lord. David said,

"Hear my cry, O God;
Attend to my prayer.
From the end of the earth I will cry to You,
When my heart is overwhelmed;
Lead me to the rock that is higher than I." (Psalm 61:1-2)

Under His Shadow Prayer

King Jesus, this morning my cry is for You to renew my heart in Your ways! Help me to always keep You before me. It is my desire to follow hard after thee! Also, Lord, I ask that you would forever keep me hungry for Your presence. Never let me be content with little I have received – but touch me so I may soar with You. Amen.

Day 30

To Do Your Will O God!

"In burnt offerings and sacrifices for sin
You had no pleasure.
Then I said, 'Behold, I have come—
In the volume of the book it is written of Me—
To do Your will, O God.'" (Hebrews 10:6, 7)

I'm amazed at how some of God's servants truly believe that by doing a bunch of good works, is enough to keep God happy in the same way it keeps us in good graces with the church.

As a matter of fact, many servants of the Lord have the idea that if they can offer some worthy sacrifice, or if they can give enough money to the collection every Sunday, that this will keep their relationship with God in good standing.

I'm not saying that doing all this is not a worthy cause or something to be acknowledged by the Lord, but doing a lot of a lot is not what God is looking for. God is not even asking for any type of sacrifice.

According to King David, he knew what sacrifices were. He understood that sacrifices were to be offered daily to the Lord. David knew however, that God was not into offerings or sacrifices!

Think about it, being that sacrifices were required by God's law to be offered daily, David could have offered countless sheep and goats! He would have offered thousands of them! He was rich; he had everything and everyone at his beck and call — he could have offered an insurmountable number of sacrifices to God – but He did not. Why not?

David didn't offer burnt offerings because he knew God, and he knew things about God that very few understood in His days. David said, "God has no pleasure in any of this."

It is almost as if in essence, David was saying, Look. I know the Lord. I know exactly what moves His heart, and goats aren't going to get it done! God is moved by the human expression found in broken hearts and willing spirits. I could give God one million goats; I could offer them night and day, or however long it would take to offer them, but God is not into it! Let me tell you what God wants from me: He wants alignment. He wants my heart, all of it; and He wants my heart to do His will! This is what is pleasing to the Lord!

From this point on, make every effort to make this your aim: To do the will of God! Not just a fraction of it, not just half of it, but all of what He is asking of you. This is what makes God smile!

Under His Shadow Prayer

Gentle Holy Spirit, please lead me this morning. I long to know Your will and Your way. Don't ever let me substitute anything for what you really want. As good as my offerings may be, you want my life pleasing you daily. Lord forgive me for the times that I have rebelled against this idea. Amen.

Day 31

The Soul Who Seeks Him!

**"The Lord is good to those who wait for Him,
To the soul who seeks Him.
It is good that one should hope and wait quietly
For the salvation of the Lord."** (Lamentations 3:25, 26)

Once again, I was captivated by His beauty as I spent sweet time in prayer and saw the Lord's awesome provision today. This is the provision that my soul always longs for!

In reading Jeremiah's lamentations, I came across this one passage where Jeremiah finally understood that the Lord eventually will do what is in His heart with His people. Though He may afflict them for a season, it won't be forever. God has an amazing plan for those He loves.

Waiting as an Action!

First, let me share with you the blessing of waiting upon

Him. Eagerly waiting for the Lord to show up, must be the hardest thing for any human being to do; yet, it has to be the most rewarding of all actions.

The opposite of waiting would probably be running. We don't get anywhere by running. Though running might advance us in bodily form, in every other area, it stifles us. If one decides to make a move because of convenience or opportunity, please understand that our hearts and minds must shift first. Waiting is internal, but running is external.

Often people only move externally, and never make the shift, internally. This action in turn, makes us wonder if we made the right move or not. Spiritual people understand this law.

Resorting to God!

Also, Jeremiah adds that God is good to the soul that seeks Him. The Hebrew understanding here is that those who seek God are really resorting to Him for an answer or a breakthrough. Do you see this?

Those who are waiting upon the Lord aren't just waiting without aim; they are waiting with the expectation that God Himself will deliver them a glorious breakthrough.

Finally, those who wait, must wait silently or quietly before Him. The attitude here is one of knowing and having confidence that as you wait upon the Lord, the answer is as sure as done!

Hoping and waiting quietly before Him, is really a matter of the heart, not only of the mind. One must know in their hearts, that salvation (deliverance) comes from the Lord! The eye of the heart must be captivated by this fact. Faith is required to see this.

Ask God to unveil a deeper understanding of this to your heart. God is good!

Under His Shadow Prayer

Lord Jesus, thank you for allowing me to meet You this morning. Thank you for guarding my life through the night. I am so overjoyed knowing You! There is no one that compares to you in any way, shape, or form. I am delighted to know that if my heart waits upon You, my life will always be established! My future is set because of You, my dreams will happen as I follow You. The outcome of my pursuit of God will be rewarding, not only in this life but in the one to come! This my heart knows it very well. I love you Jesus! Amen.

Day 32

Hold Fast to Jesus!

"Let us hold fast the confession of our hope without wavering, for He who promised is faithful." (Hebrews 10:23)

How often is it that we lose heart when things don't work out for us? What happens when our expectations are not met, people might let us down, or things just go awry and we find ourselves destitute and overcome by the feeling of failure? Have you been here? I have.

Can you imagine the church of Jesus Christ in the first century? They were holding on for dear life to their faith and belief in Christ as many were being persecuted by the Roman government, and being challenged by Gnostics, Pharisees, and Sadducees, etc.

I don't mean to be disrespectful or sound uncaring, but we must revisit our motives for the way we get discouraged in our time.

You see, many of these servants of God had to fight through soldiers and adverse situations to get to a prayer meeting. No wonder whenever they thanked God, it truly meant something to them!

Unlike today, many believers are easily swayed and discouraged by the smallest things such as: "the pastor didn't shake my hand, so I'm not coming back to church," or "I am too tired from work, I can't come to prayer tonight," or "They will not promote me at work! I am just so overwhelmed and can't focus on Jesus right now! I am sure there are countless more of lame excuses for not making it to the prayer meeting.

I say all that to say this: Every expectation that we have had, we must ask ourselves, Did the Lord make that promise to me personally, or is it something that I really want and I'm confusing it with 'the Lord told me he was going to do this for me,' promise?

I am not sure about all the spiritual hang-ups people have, but one thing I know is that I must set my eyes on Jesus and not waver in my devotion to Him. I must persevere in Him!

As far as expectations go, I have learned that if God didn't give them to me, I won't just invent something out of my empty head. It has never worked out for me the many times I tried to convince myself that it was God, when I knew well in my heart that it was not!

Under His Shadow Prayer

Good morning, King Jesus! I am so delighted to be in Your awesome presence this morning. It has been quite a ride going through this protracted fast, but I feel such nearness to You — I will trade my encounters with You for food anytime! Today, I want to acknowledge You as my Keeper! You have kept me going through the good, the bad and the ugly moments in my life. All I know is that, with every storm that passes, I grow. I keep falling in love with You over and over and over again! Thank You for being You! Amen.

Day 33

A Rewarding Confidence!

"Therefore do not cast away your confidence, which has great reward. For you have need of endurance, so that after you have done the will of God, you may receive the promise." (Hebrews 10:34-36)

This morning as I was prostrated before the Lord, I read this portion of Scripture in Hebrews, and began to ponder the suffering of these servants of God.

It was perhaps one of the most dangerous times to be a believer and part of a church group. Anyone who was involved with them, more than likely, would face repercussions for their faith—o giving up was probably a more convenient thing to do.

Yet, in all these battles the apostles kept encouraging the church to be strong and to keep pressing on for Jesus.

Pressing on for Jesus!

Often in our walk with the Lord, we will face countless discouragements. What do you do? What does anyone do when their expectations are not met and everything just seems to go sour? Here's what I do:

Get Perspective. Before I go and do something stupid, I will take the setback, or the unfulfilled expectation, and bring it before the Lord in prayer. I need perspective of my life, not of my situation. I need to know where I stand under God's umbrella. Am I holding on to the hand of God? Am I trusting God with my life and future? The answer is very telling of my perspective. Is anything making a great attempt to move me from where God placed me that would be in Him?

If I know that there is no known sin in my life, and things are fine between my heavenly Father and I— then all I must do is worship. In the case that I know that there is sin in my life, then I must repent of it before the Lord before doing anything else. After this, I will spend time in His presence and allow Him to embrace me as I am.

Did I say that this is not an easy thing to do?

After a failure, a setback, or an unfulfilled expectation is not met, all you want to do is hide, cry, and scream. The flesh wants you to worry instead of worship. Don't let this happen to you. Again, it is not easy to do, but it is not impossible to do either!

Enter into the Fields of Praise!

When things look dim, just praise Him . . .

To praise God is to call attention to His glory. Acknowledge His majesty and bless the Lord for all He has done. Thank Him for all the opportunities to grow in Him. Exalt His name because He alone is worthy to be praised for all His goodness to you. Know that the heartbreaks of life are only opportunities to praise and love on Him!

A Rewarding Confidence

Finally, you must know that your confidence has a great reward attached to it. Have the boldness to stand until the answer comes. Learn the art of endurance and stay put! Don't let your emotions run your life. Don't allow your situation to change who or what the Lord has meant to you, and don't allow yourself to be seduced into quitting!

Under His Shadow Prayer

King Jesus, once again I am here in Your sweet presence. Help me to process my life in the light of You — not in the light of anything that has gone wrong. You are still the King of my life and there is no other. I will not doubt, fear, or run away from Your presence. I will allow this difficulty to break me and refine me. Afterwards, I know I will stand victorious — for You will make me stand! Amen.

Day 34

Acceptable Content!

"By faith Enoch was taken away so that he did not see death, 'and was not found, because God had taken him,' for before he was taken he had this testimony, that he pleased God." (Hebrews 11:5)

This morning, I came across this passage and it so blessed me that I want to share it with you as you venture out into a new day. You know, when our hearts are hungry for revelation of His nature, He opens the heavens and enables us to see beyond the veil.

As I prayed and meditated, I came across the life of Enoch. Not much is said about the man, but it is enough to move my heart towards God. Sometimes, God will allow us to see only what really matters and not much more than that.

The Bible says that Enoch was taken by the Lord— I'm assuming this means that he was carried away and never seen again by the Lord. This is somewhat of a strange event. Nevertheless, it is a prophetic picture of all those who walk with God — those who are always longing to draw near and keep climbing higher in the Spirit.

What I want you to see first, is how a man or woman of God who walks in the Spirit, soars to higher levels in God, and although they are here on earth, they always appear to be taken into another realm or another dimension.

Enoch was literally taken with God. There is no error in this. I mean, they looked for him and couldn't find him. Due to his nearness to God, everyone concluded that God had taken him.

Now, the Scripture says something very deep about this man. It reads like this, **"...for before he was taken he had this testimony, that he pleased God."**

Regarding his life, one thing surely stood out, **"he pleased God."**

What does pleasing God mean? Well, I did some research on this and discovered one of the greatest truths I have ever seen in Scripture. To please God, means acceptable content.

In other words, Enoch was a man who heard from God and allowed God to deposit in him acceptable content. Enoch became a carrier of acceptable content.

Now, please tell me, how can God not trust a man who believes in Him and yields himself fully to Him with everything in his life? Is it any wonder, why God would take him?

We must make it our aim to be servants of God who allow God to deposit acceptable content in us, and then live out this content so we may please Him! Let us position ourselves to be ready to hear and ready to run with whatever He tells us to do.

Under His Shadow Prayer

Lord Jesus, this morning, I fully yielded myself to know You. Whatever the cost, whatever the sacrifice, Lord, I'll pay it. I want to know Your heart in all matters; I want to understand Your ways in a deeper way! Amen.

Day 35

Can't Please Him, If...

"But without faith it is impossible to please Him, for he who comes to God must believe that He is, and that He is a rewarder of those who diligently seek Him." (Hebrews 11:6)

Faith is the key to knowing God's economy. We will never know anything about God and His purposes for us, until we enter the realm of faith.

When it comes to faith, you can't chase it down, you can't manipulate it, you can't wish for it, you can't beg for it. Faith is not running — faith is resting in God. I know too many times people say, "I need more faith!" or "Pray for me so that God would give me enough faith to conquer this huge mountain before me."

My friends, faith comes by resting and by knowing that God is. That is all.

Though we can't see with our natural eye or feel anything with our natural senses, the eyes, and ears of the heart, by faith, will capture the heavenly picture and download it to our natural faculties so that we may act on what we are being told by our Spirit.

Without Faith?

Now without faith following the Lord is impossible! Being that God is Spirit and those who attempt to follow Him must do so by the same Spirit— there is no real way of following God in the Spirit if we can't sense the Spirit of God moving.

The person who follows the Lord must do it believing that God is!

Must Believe!

Faith takes us behind the idea that says, Are you sure there is a God? In our natural mind, we may wonder if there is a God, and our mind may play games with our thinking and challenge our convictions.

Now, if faith is in its proper place — all doubt and unbelief, every argument and opposing ideas will be demolished by

His Spirit.

Faith takes us behind the veil and allows us to see God as He is. We can potentially experience as much of God as we desire. We can do the works of God upon the earth through faith. Signs and wonders can follow us, if we would only believe— this is the faith of God at work.

Rewarded!

Also, if one moves by faith and believes that God is, the Scripture says that we will be rewarded for this. In other words, God is not going to make a fool out of anybody. He will keep His words to us every time, so long as faith is what is in operation in our soul.

If we diligently seek Him, He will reward us. You see, it is faith that allows us to move with God's ideas and God always blesses His ideas carried out by us!

Under His Shadow Prayer

Oh! wow Jesus, this morning, my heart is so overwhelmed with Your beauty. Your promises for me are awesome. You said that if I would simply believe, you could do anything in me and through me. Lord, help me to walk out this real faith. Help me to make it my aim to please You always! Amen.

Day 36

I Know What the Promise is Not!

"By faith Abraham obeyed when he was called to go out to the place which he would receive as an inheritance. And he went out, not knowing where he was going. By faith he dwelt in the land of promise as in a foreign country, dwelling in tents with Isaac and Jacob, the heirs with him of the same promise; for he waited for the city which has foundations, whose builder and maker is God." (Hebrews 11:8-10)

Moving by faith is the secret to moving in the Lord. When we trust God with His promises, His personal words, or prophetic dreams, we will end up at the right place at the right time.

It is interesting to see how Abraham obeyed the Lord when he was called to go to the place that he would receive as an inheritance. He did this without knowing what the outcome would be—or did he? Did Abraham have any type of inclination where God might be taking him?

In the Scripture it says that **"...he went out, not knowing where he was going."**

But knew enough to know where he was not supposed to be! As a matter of fact, the Scripture says, **"...he waited for the city which has foundations, whose builder and maker is God."**

Knowing in our hearts what God wants from us is key! When we know what God desires, will protect us from going astray. It will keep us from pursuing a false and fleshly dream.

So Abraham Lived his life as directed by God, and he waited for this promise to play out. This had to take a lot of discipline tremendous perseverance. It is not easy playing second fiddle to anything. It is not easy following the leader— but Abraham did it. He didn't become exasperated with God (that we know of) or overcome by his own desires and wishes.

He knew all too well what God wanted to accomplish, so he didn't settle for second best, **"he waited for the city which has foundations, whose builder and maker is God."**

I must ask: In your own life, are you waiting for God's best? Or are you overcome by your own fleshly desires and keep jumping the gun at every opportunity presented?

Let me close this meditation by reiterating that Abraham might not have known the whole plan as laid out by the Lord, but he did know what it was not! Can we discern in our own lives what it is that God doesn't want?

Under His Shadow Prayer

Holy Spirit, please take me higher. I want to be like Abraham— who might not have known all the details about the promise given to him, but he kept waiting and waiting until the true foundation appeared. This is where I want to be with you Jesus! Teach me to discern Your wishes. Amen.

Day 37

When God Begs to Differ!

"Therefore, from one man, and him as good as dead, were born as many as the stars of the sky in multitude—innumerable as the sand which is by the seashore." (Hebrews 11:12)

When we think of hopelessness or ridiculousness, we must look to the Lord for all these things to make sense. It seems that only the Lord can put these things in proper order and make them work. Yes, only God can make sense of impossible things. What is impossible for man is possible for God!

I want to take you behind the scenes in the life of Abraham and see how his life applies so much to ours today.

God made this man an awesome promise. You see, God needed a nation built, so He chose a man that would get it done — his name was Abraham. He took Abraham out of his own country and out of his own comfort zone and moved him to a place where God would show him later.

God made him a promise. The promise was that Abraham would be great and that his lineage would multiply and that through him, he would bless the world in a great way. God promised him and his children abundance and blessing for the rest of their days.

The promise was made when Abraham was 75 years of age. I mean, he wasn't young when this promise was made, so time was of the essence— at least, that is how many would perceive it to be.

Now, God is not in any hurry. He is always patient and takes His time to unfold His wisdom.

Anyone who is a recipient of God's promises must budget in the time of a promise fulfilled. Sometimes, promises do happen quickly. Other times, they happen in a few days, weeks, or months, but rarely does a promise take longer. Well, this is not the case in Abraham's life.

In Abraham's life, the promise had already taken more than 25 years. This is a long time to wait for something, but Abraham somehow pulled it off, of course, after committing a grave mistake!

Now, 25 years have passed, and the promise is still yet to come, but, there is a slight problem— Abraham is too old to have children, or is he? Well, God doesn't think so!

This argument would go on and on, but God settled the matter in His way and made the promise come to pass no matter what anyone thought. No one's opinion mattered: not Abraham's, not Sarah's, no one's!

That is why the Scripture says, **"Therefore from one man, and him as good as dead, were born as many as the stars of the sky in multitude—innumerable as the sand which is by the seashore."**

God will do the same with you and me; when God gets good and ready to fulfill His promise to you and I, He will get it done in His way and in His time!

Under His Shadow Prayer

My Lord, please forgive me for being selfish. Forgive me for being so demanding and making the attempt to fulfill my own destiny without your leadership. I repent for my ways and embrace Yours! Thank You Holy Spirit for leading me with Your word! Amen.

Day 38

A Tool, An Experience, or A Passion?

"And do not be conformed to this world [any longer with its superficial values and customs] **but be transformed and progressively changed** [as you mature spiritually] **by the renewing of your mind** [focusing on godly values and ethical attitudes], **so that you may prove** [for yourselves] **what the will of God is, that which is good and acceptable and perfect** [in His plan and purpose for you]." (Romans 12:2 -AMP)

While in meditation this morning— the Holy Spirit started speaking to me regarding the things we do as humans such as exercising, studying, eating, praying, and many other things we like to do for our hobbies.

I asked the Lord why He was speaking to me about these things. He proceeded to show me how some things are done because they are needed, (they are tools) other things we do for the experience, (we enjoy them) and finally, some things we do for the passion (we love them).

I thought it was interesting to hear God speak of such matters, so I began to question Him.

The Tools

I asked the Lord what He meant by tools. He said to me, Tools are simply things that help us get a job done. We don't enjoy using a hammer, (as an experience) and most of us are not passionate about banging nails on wood. There may be some exceptions, but for the most part, it only serves to get a job done.

The Experience

Now, some people, when working out, enjoy the experience of going to a gym or being there to see other people exercise. To them just working out to only work out doesn't seem fun, and it really doesn't bring in a good experience. Obviously, these people will pay the monthly membership fee, drive for miles to get to the gym and spend long hours experiencing the wonderful machines. To them exercise is more than just a tool— it's an experience!

The Passionate Heart

Then we have the third level of appreciation. Many people like running or jogging for the sake of losing weight and distressing. Running or jogging is a big part of what they do to tackle these rudiments. Some people may see this simply as a tool. Then you have the other tribe, the ones who run with a timer, buy the latest sportswear and running shoes, who are conscious of calories, heart rate, and distance. These people enjoy the whole experience of running or jogging. Even still, there are others putting on their gear, their sports watch,, get in their car and head to the hills maybe 10 or 15 miles away to enjoy the morning dew, the sunrise, the fresh wind, the rough terrain, or the mountain trails, etc. Now this is a passionate heart in action!

I asked the Lord why He was showing me the different levels of appreciation and He said to me, David, this is how I want you to discern your life with Me!

So, as I close this meditation today, I would love for you to ask yourself this honest question: What is the Lord to you? Is he only a tool to get what you want or need? Or perhaps just a feel good experience when you are feeling alone or overwhelmed? Or is He a passion that makes you set aside all other loves in exchange for Him?

Under His Shadow Prayer

Jesus, help me to walk in this discernment. I want to know what things rule my heart daily. Help me to always follow hard after thee! Amen.

Day 39

Can You See Him Who Is Invisible?

"By faith he forsook Egypt, not fearing the wrath of the king; for he endured as seeing Him who is invisible." (Hebrews 11:27)

In seeing the life of Moses and studying some of what he accomplished while serving the Pharaoh, one has to say that it was amazing how God led and directed his steps.

Now, Moses' life was not an easy breezy life, even if it may appear that way. Remember, he was exalted by God to end at the right hand of Pharaoh. It wasn't simply Moses working it all out in his own ability and strength.

Living for Pharaoh.

Let me give you a quick synopsis of this man's adventure in Egypt: He first came to Egypt through a miracle and was born to a Hebrew mother. At the time, all male Hebrew children were in danger of being killed in the name of Pharaoh. Anyone with spiritual discernment would be able to tell you that this was the work of the devil himself!

In all this, God protected Moses: first, as a baby, then as an adolescent, and finally as an adult.

Here's what we know: Moses knew deep within his heart that he was born for so much more. He felt his life had a different purpose than just being a leader in Egypt. He soon discovered God had a plan for him, and knew in his heart that he would follow Him. It wasn't going to be easy but God helped him get to that point.

Living for Jehovah God.

Soon after maturing, he recognized that he didn't want to be associated with Pharaoh or the lifestyle of Egyptians. He then opened his heart to follow the ways of the Lord.

These actions had to do with being the deliverer of God's people from Egyptian bondage. In doing this, he had to step out in faith believing that this was what God wanted him to do. Confronting Pharaoh was difficult, but Moses had been anointed and was not afraid of the outcome.

Positioning oneself under the direction of God is not an easy thing to do. You must be fully convinced that this is what God wants and pursue it until you reach it. Moses, **"forsook Egypt, not fearing the wrath of the king; for he endured as seeing Him who is invisible."**

One must see Christ before He can do what is in God's heart. If this doesn't happen, don't make a move! If you make a move without God leading you, it can be extremely detrimental to you and those around you. This is wisdom speaking.

Under His Shadow Prayer

Lord Jesus, this morning I yield myself to You once again. I understand Your divine order in matters of Your perfect will. I don't want to do anything that comes from my own head — I don't want to be an ideas man. I want to be inspired by Your Spirit and be guided by Him. Help me to live my life with a passion to please only You! Amen.

Day 40

God's Watchman!

"Now it came to pass at the end of seven days that the word of the Lord came to me, saying, 'Son of man, I have made you a watchman for the house of Israel; therefore, hear a word from My mouth, and give them warning from Me.'" (Ezekiel 3:16-17)

What is a watchman?

A watchman is someone who keeps watch— someone on the lookout. Watchmen were servants of the king who would be placed on towers to keep their eyes open for any foreign enemy that might come into the city to cause trouble.

Much responsibility was placed on them— thus they needed to always be on high alert.

What does the watchman do?

Watchmen were called to keep an eye out for oncoming danger. The enemy was always making an effort to enter cities and disrupt, therefore watchmen were placed in strategic locations to keep guard day and night.

Now, the watchman couldn't afford to fall asleep whenever they felt like it. You see, the watchman was the greatest voice of defense against the enemy. The walls of the city were meant to protect enemy forces, but the watchman would alert the soldiers to the approaching danger, and they needed to be ready for war!

If the watchman fell asleep, many lives could be lost. Not only soldiers would die, but women and children as well. Along with families, the whole culture of what had been established would be changed or annihilated.

Spiritual Watchman

Just like in nature, God has also raised watchmen all over His body, His church, the spiritual watchman. It is the Lord's intent to keep His church protected by placing guards on its towers; those guards could be anyone who wants to hear God and be held responsible or accountable for speaking His prophetic word to the church.

Not everyone desires this responsibility, but many have been called by God to do this type of work.

I believe that the Lord wants all of us to be a type of watchman in our personal world.

I believe that every person or single parent should be the watchman over their own family; I believe that every person who holds a responsibility or a high office at their place of employment, should also be a watchman for God.

This is the method that God uses to keep His church flowing in a dark and compromising world. You and I have been called to be God's watchman.

Under His Shadow Prayer

King Jesus, please let me serve You in any way I can. I want to be a true servant who sees and walks in the spirit. I want to glorify Your Name everywhere I go and in every little thing I do. Please keep me marching forward and prophesying as many times as I need to, and may I form part of that group that brings Your glory into the earth. Amen.

Ministry Information

Shabar Publications is a ministry expression under Masterbuilder Ministries, Inc. in Palmhurst, Texas. This publication ministry, was founded and created for the purpose of writing books and distributing them to the body of Christ both locally and globally. The intent behind the idea of publishing these works, is to train and equip the reader to be a more intimate lover of Jesus Christ, our Lord! Out of an intimate life with God, by the grace of God, effective ministry will be the outflow.

For more information regarding this ministry, feel free to email us at: mayorga1126@gmail.com.

Printed by Libri Plureos GmbH in Hamburg, Germany